In

This book is dedicated to my grandmother, Darlene Tucker, and my best friend and furry son, Denver. Both passed away in the several months before I began working on this book. Without them, their love, and their unwavering support I would not be writing this today.

I love you both.

-Craig Firsdon

A Requiem For Grandma

As the sun goes down
and the cold December winds
whip through trees rattling branches
like chattering of teeth on shivering trunks
i focus on placing these words down
on this small screen to remember you.

I try to focus through grief
and realize the memories are too many
and the love is so deep,
Some thoughts separate themselves from the myriad
and begin to slowly show themselves to me clearly.
I am trying hard to relay them
but nothing fancy or creative seems to come to mind.
All that does is simply this:
I love you.
I miss you.

I can and will always remember and appreciate you
for all that you have done for me.

You kept me warm in these cold winds
in a way no fire ever could.
You became the requiem to
my dreams,
my hopes,
my everything.

Simply you were and will eternally be
my forever,
my always.

REQUIEM

By

Craig Firsdon

Cover design by Craig Firsdon

Table Of Contents
(Title – Page)

❖ **A Dedication**
Requiem For Grandma (2014)

❖ **A Message**
My People (2016)

1. **By Order**

2. **In Order By Category**

• **Poems Of Myself:**

Myself

A Message

This book has been many years in the making and in that time the world has changed a lot. Just turn on the tv and you will see terrorist attacks, police shootings, riots and all forms of hate. As a result prejudice has prevailed, even when the intended result was the opposite. We see races and religions shouting their people matter with the intended result being the strengthening of their people, but in reality what occurs is isolation and racism. Because of this I wanted to show not only that other groups, like my people the disabled, have been hurt as much if not more, but mainly (and most importantly) that all lives matter. We all need peace, love and unity within ourselves and with each other. I hope everyone can take something from this poem and pass it on to others. #AllLivesMatter

My People (All Lives Matter)

Since the beginning of recorded history,
my people have been the target
of hate and prejudice
without a single reparation paid
and sparse laws passed that
are laughable and rarely enforced.

My people were made to work
when they seldom were able,
otherwise my people were placed
into small overcrowded buildings
and left to rot and die.

My people were victims
of the Holocaust,
experimented on and extinguished.
My people were segregated,
castrated, euthanized and lobotomized
by the Holy Roman Empire, the Nazis,

and countries from pre-medieval to modern times
all across the world from Russia
to the good old U S of A.

My people have been cursed at,
put down and hated by all
sexes, colors, races, religions and creeds.
My people comes from everywhere,
we are white, black, Asian
and every other color,
we believe in all beliefs
and have shed tears in every language.
My people cry hard and die early
but live and love just as every other person
on this planet does.

My people have overcome
to become leaders and presidents,
world changing scientists,
lifesaving soldiers and doctors
and award winning entertainers and writers.

My people are the disabled, the handicapped.
The lives we were given were not of our choice
and the hardships we have
been put through over the centuries
have broken many of us
and strengthened the rest.
We have suffered as much
as all other peoples.

In the end one truth can be learned
from the lives of every peoples
across this vast planet:
WE matter,
ALL people matter,
ALL LIVES matter

R equiem

Poetry is something special to me. It is what I feel, what I dream, why I wake up. Poetry has healed me and taken away pain as well as, or if not better, than any prescription drug. I am disabled. What I have is called juvenile rheumatoid arthritis or JRA. I haven't walked since I was 12. I have both knees, my right hip and elbow all replaced and a pain pump inside of me. Through everything what gave me an outlet to deal with the pain, inabilities, prejudice and much more was poetry. These poems are a compilation of past and present poems that express the real me, who I am, what I believe, why I write, my life, my dreams, my past, present and future. I hope this poetry, and poetry in general, can be a special part of your life, like it is mine. So speak up. Whether you read a poem, sing a song or write a story, let everyone know you are here.

This first poem is about the first time I really wrote a poem, one I put all of myself into and, because of this, launched me into the world of poetry. On February 14, 1997 my grandfather passed away. At that time it was the hardest thing I'd ever dealt with. The day of the funeral I was asked to write a poem to be read during the eulogy. I did so quickly, but for the first time I really put my very soul into a poem. This was the day poetry was born for me and this is about that poem.

The Day Poetry Was Born

In '97 I said good bye to him
by looking through tear blinded eyes
into a sky washed with grey
and kaleidoscope coffin clouds.

I never saw him that "one last time"
A whisker covered smile was etched

into my memories of a man I called grandpa.
A man with a love for cough drops
who could go on and on telling stories
often sprinkled with expletives
and spoken with a raspy voice
that screamed tobacco smoker and West Virginia.
I had last seen him a month before that day
but that month felt like an eternity to me
and in that eternity I could have told him
that I loved him forever an always
                    one last time,
that I was just as proud of him
                    as he was of me,
that he was, still is, and will always be
                    a hero, my hero.

Before I could say a last goodbye
he would change my life one last time.
The day of the service I was asked
to put pen to paper,
turn my tears into words
and write my first poem,
read to an audience...
my soldier, my hero, my grandpa.

Inside of me that was the day
poetry was born.

Reflection Of A Poet

Fame is an idea,
A singular concept,
that we place upon others
out of our insecurities
in what we are now,
   what we wish we had accomplished,
   and what we, as individuals
   want to become.

Fame is not false idols,
   is not money,
   although it helps.
No, fame is coveted greed
for what the almighty dollar represents:
      power,
      hope,
      justice,
      fear,
      strength.
The invisible ego
speaking in the back of our minds,
   the sheep in wolf's clothing.

I am a poet.
I use words as thread
to sew the truth
on the lapel of society.
The scarlet letter painted
on each and everyone
in blood drawn by letters
spoken as my words.
The blood that is life.
Life flows through poetry.
The poet is a warrior

slashing with words
opening wounds that need to bleed
to slay the fame monster.
I am a warrior,
I am a poet
and this life I lead
flows through poetry.

In The Moment

When I write poetry
putting pen to paper,
finger to keyboard,
times pauses for the moment
(tick tock tick...)
and my world stops spinning.

In that brief micro-chasm of time pain ceases,
stock markets crash through glass floors
without making a single sound,
the heartless corrupt the mindless
with green backs and fool's gold,
frozen gazes set on false idols and altars
and I begin to think..

I see inner city kids imprisoned
in jails while sporting colors,
red for "help me",
blue for "save me",
and confined in communities they call their ghettos
not to be confused with Hitler's confines
both equally damning,
both equally self-torturing,
both equally wrong.

When it comes to those that have,
their money flows alongside blood and sweat.
I am still surprised
to see entrepreneurs go to school for business degrees
to get a dream job that will stay a dream
and a Barbie doll wife,
all tits and no substance,
only to achieve nothing
and lose everything.

It is not freedom,
or the lack of freedom,
that is to blame.
Freedom is a smoke screen
and as the light of day beats down,
slaying shadows in the moment,
it slowly evaporates
a little more each passing minute of our lives.
But even in death freedom has disappeared.
St. Peter has just installed scanners at Heaven's Gates.
Maybe I'm not going to Heaven after all.

See when I write poems
I live in the moment,
I see into the future
and learn from the past.

The Road

The road between pain and peace,
one littered with the potholes
of anguish and struggle.
This road called life,
traveled an infinite number of times,

worn away by the feet of all of those
before and still to come.

Walking, I remember every stone,
every rounded, marbled piece of gravel.
The smallest, and most seemingly inconsequential,
I remember the best
because they are the ones that
gave me hope and propelled me
out of the holes I fall in,
over the hills of struggle
and toward our desired destination;
The freedoms to love unequivocally,
hope immeasurably and the strength
and guidance to lead even the unable
through every road way journeyed.

It is the journey that makes us who we are;
More than human, more than soul.
We are the journey.
We are every road we travel.
We are every person we meet;
we are every stone and pebble,
Every blade of grass that is dispersed
amongst the cracks we trip in.

Traveling toward the journey's end
looking inside we see our hearts
beating in symphony with the tides,
our souls blazing brighter than any supernova.
Both, heart and soul, knowing the truth
of that which we are,
always have been
and always will be,
And that is simply:

We are everything;
Past, present, future.
We are
  Whole.

Stronger Than Superman

I.
Dreaming of the superhero I once was.
As a child I would put on superman pajamas,
pin a towel on my back
and pretend it's a red cape.
Wishing it were soaring through the sky
like riding on a magic carpet.
I'd run around the house jumping
off furniture, gliding as if I were a kite
with the cape flowing behind me fluidly.
I was a superhero with super powers
and in my mind I was truly free.
Months later things changed.
My ankles began to hurt and turn in.
Later my neck ached.
Then that and my arms and legs stiffened.
I was only four and my life began to change.
This Superman found his kryptonite
and it was ravaging his body.

II.
"Leukemia!" they screamed.
The Luthorian doctors were eager to name my kryptonite.
They didn't know what it was and to be honest
most of the time they didn't seem to care.
Time passed and my kryptonite was found.
It was juvenile rheumatoid arthritis.

My body was attacking itself.
I was given chemicals,
almost every type of medication.
Even gold filled my veins.
No matter the treatment
the outcome was always the same.
I was no longer Superman
and never would be again.

III.
From then on I was forever human
feeling pain and misery and sometimes
even the glimmering of hope would cross my mind.
Every day I have fought.
Scars now cross my skin
and titanium has become a part of me,
but I have become stronger than I ever thought possible.
Stronger than a superhero.
Stronger than a Superman.

Flight Of A Private Manifest Destiny

Sometimes I wish I could fly away,
I wish I could leave my body,
leave my soul,
leave who I am
and what I'm to become.
I'd spontaneously combust
into something more,
something greater,
a blessing and a curse,
a dream amongst nightmares.

I'd drift from this very seat,

meld trough the ceiling
and take my place in the sky
parting clouds,
waiving to angels
and stealing their halos
for my collection of shiny things.

I'd take a page from Hal Jordan
and soar on constructs
of Vicodin and hope,
which I'd forge into a bird
with two left wings
flying with a Percocet hangover.

Skyward dreaming
my veins are being flooded.
Life returning, transported through pain,
filling with the whirring pump
screaming constantly for more.

Life glides by
all the while we just sit there
listening to news
that barely fits the airwaves
from ear buds in economy class seating
without parachutes.
These one-way pa systems
warning of gulf oil gasoline
driving broken motors
repaired with the best
monkey wrenches money can buy.

Falling to earth,
an archangel on acid,
fueled by privatized life support systems
becomes a laugh track.

As if it matters to magistrates,
who close their eyes
as their subjects crash,
content in kaleidoscope dreams
and neo-Nazi smurf nightmares.

Returning, closed eyes
cause today to fade into tomorrow
as it all comes full circle
taking off on two left wings
and flying into another
private manifest destiny.

Internal Thoughts

I wish I could be the happy poet here.
I could write something inspirational
and scribble down words of encouragement,
Or give all the bullshitters in the world
a big old middle finger F U.
If only I could,
but right now I can't.
I am lost.
My compass is broken.

As I write this here in my birthplace,
a small city in northwest Ohio
where truth is welcomed by silence
filling the airwaves with scripted nothingness,
I am content surrounded by my family,
kin by both blood and ink,
and a library of books written
in black and white
that read shades of gray.

But yet, still I feel homesick
for a place I'm not sure even exists.
And all I need is a push.
An opportunity.
A one-way ticket.
Something.

But whatever that something is
I can never seem to reach it.
I'm falling apart at the seems.
My strings are breaking.
My insides are coming loose.
My buttons don't button.
My zippers don't zip.
And the fakest smile I can fake,
Isn't fake enough.

In Words

I write to share
with you in the only
way I know how:
in words,
in lines,
in poems
formed
by the music
in my soul.

My songs start
as letters,
as syllables,
placed together to
form messages of

truth and freedom,
of life,
of society,
of what we were,
who we are
and what we can be.

So when I sing my
messages
I do so in a silent voice
in the hope that
you may hear
what others don't
and what I try to but
do not
and
can not
speak.
Now, in looking back
and gazing forward
I come to the conclusion
which is simply:
For those that
do not listen
I'm sorry.
For those that
do listen
Thank you.

Welcome

Welcome to the present.
There are no rules in this.
We make them up as we go

and even then they are tentative at best.
It seems more like boundaries, invisible lines.
Some we cross and re-cross.
Yet others we must respect and admire.

It's not like there are an abundant
amount of chances here.
Opportunities, yes,
if you are lucky enough to get them.
So then things like life and morality
become more like a code to live by:
musts, must-nots,
shoulds, should-nots.

If we wish to persevere,
we push and ultimately we suffer.
Isn't it better to suffer with purpose
and live with intent
all the while seizing life with
a kind of awe inspired grip
that makes life rue the day
it thought acceptable to offer
you lemons in place of EVERYTHING!
Or will life be the one left laughing
because we are too fretful
to see the totality of it all.

Another Jackson Pollock

Making art can't be difficult:
if it looks like nothing
it must be good and
if it looks like something
then it would be a photograph.

I would like to study art
and then do it all wrong,
like painting Vincent
missing the wrong ear
or have Mona Lisa
wink at me.

I'd be another
Jackson Pollock
and maybe I'd silkscreen
cans of soup.
Only not full ones
but empty ones with
their jagged lids sticking up
because that's how the
world has moved on.

And the lids wouldn't
be modern pull rings
but the old kind you have
to open with a can opener.
It would refer back
to another time and be
a metaphor for
everything lost
and how everything
should be.

The Artist or Tinkering With Words Of Freedom

I guess "they" feel to be an artist,
be it words, paints, pencils or clay,
you must be a genius,
dripping knowledge from your pencil,

from your brush, from the very pores of your fingertips...
Your medium can never be medium.
Their eyes mumble,
closed and pursed.

The whispers from them are deafening
and test the belief I have in myself.
Sometimes "they" speak to me
with whispers rattling my eardrums.
"They" say "to be a great artist is to know everything"
but "everything" only exists in their world,
a projected reality based fantasy
populated with caged artists 'they" have enslaved.

These artists wave shackled hands
across a page of poetic words,
upon a canvas of blood born colors,
over damp dough like earth polluted with broken passion,
abrasive to the touch,
each conveying a simple message:
There is never a great artist.
There is never a good artist.
There is never a normal or adequate artist.
There is, however, horrible artists,
understandable but meaningless,
coming from the mouths of "they"
and not the passion born of themselves.

Something artists will never fully be known as?
Adored.
Respected.
Wanted.
Instead words become arms races
and colors become battle cries
to wars ending silently in reluctant compliance...
thrown out..

only to go right back in across the mine fields
of rash comments on how their poetry lacks intelligence
or how they need to work a little more.
Desecrating charcoal and color reflections
into shards of nothingness
when they had worked so hard already
only to be tied down
and break free,
tied down
and break free.

When we shed our ties that bind
we create unbound art.
It still may be called worthless
trash
scarred
thrown out
and yet these same words
can be what changes the world.

Beautiful Pictures

Beautiful pictures
painted in red.
Still wet,
undefined,
unfinished.
Ready to be as wished.

The paint spills new places.
Sometimes more goes on the canvas.
Sometimes it drips to the floor.

The pools then become form,
an art form newly born,
and given breath by accident and free will.

Such a talented painter,
but no one can know.
All work must be concealed
from those who don't understand.
Even from those who may and should.
Concealed from all,
hidden from the world.

Aged with beautiful skill,
they say painters are crazy,
not to be trusted or believed,
but they are just misunderstood.
Strengthened by persecution
and kept alive by overcoming contempt.
Unlike others, their paint is formed beneath their skin.

The paint never stays.
Eventually it washes away.
Another painter dead and gone,
but the memories of their works
and the imprints left on the world
are always and forever.

Beautiful pictures,
Painted in red.
Now dry,
perfect,
finished.
As they were meant to be.

Truth of "Me"

Pen and ink have always known me.
Through blood, sweat and pain
my words are written in both
joyous and painful tears.
Tears that become poems,
that become self-evident truths.
My life through my eyes,
my book is slowly being written.
So if you want to find me
I'll be amongst folded pages
where my naked emotions lay bare
and my freedom is truly free.

Boots Of Lead

I've said so much
in all of my writings.
I should probably stop.
Really, my life
truly
isn't that interesting.
My fumbling attempts
to express
represent only a small fraction
of my thoughts.
If I were to let them all flow,
my words would be
garbled.
I would drown
and my mind

would continue
pouring them out.
Raining,
pouring from the spigots
of these fingertips.
The thing is
I'm just going through the struggle.
Same as many others
and most poets.
I take one day at a time.
One word,
one step,
plodding along
in these boots of lead.

Diamond

It takes a lot for dirt
to become a diamond.
The greater the pressure in our lives,
the more pain dealt upon us with each day gone by,
the farther we have to reach
   and grasp what we deserve,
the more beautiful of a human being
   we become in the end.
Every fallen drop of blood
and every bead of sweat shed
when life hits us the hardest,
when fear scares us too much to stand for ourselves,
when words are spoken
   that slice us like razors

and stab us like daggers,
molds the dirt like clay between fingertips
and presses it until finally
we become flawed perfection,
a diamond.

In Time

the way eyes always stare
at my shell, my body,
at my broken side,
must be meant to be
unseen.

this circus side show,
geometric abstraction of a form
past it's never existed prime,
warranty expired,
to be stripped for parts.
eventually.
maybe.
most likely
just shipped to the junkyard cemetery
buried alongside the other defectives
or quickly oven-smelted,
if lucky.

we are told over and over again
like fusion flame seared into our minds,
that the inevitable will happen.
only rely on it and taxes
to become a reality.

the inevitability is killing me,

really.
"It'll be your time when it is meant to be"
i don't wear a watch, never have,
and the only time piece in my possession
lays in my drawer, broken,
unable to tell me what the "time" is.

a broken time-harnessed body
laying in a coffin not of its making
waiting to be fixed.
knowing it never will,
yet never wanting it to happen.

I Believed In Superheroes

Early evening.
Sitting at the dining room table
flipping through a comic book,
page by page from first to last.
Reading into hidden nuances
on pages that become less visible with age
and as addicting as Ritalin to a child.

I remember dreaming
of being a superhero
to conquer all super villains and monsters
in my own life and the lives of those
I call my family or friends.

Sometimes I'd dream of being Superman,
my powers many and weaknesses few.
During the day my alter ego enjoying life
with my brothers and mother, my family
smiling, laughing, perception set as mirrors

reflecting truth and what it is like to be free.
As night falls I meld my being into Superman
to brace myself for what's to come
as my dad rolls into our driveway slowly,
taking his time
to get the crazy juices
flowing within himself.

I feel I should have stopped my father
from verbally and mentally hurting us,
from his schizoid personality disorder,
from becoming a broken man.
Yes, I could have stopped him,
let his words bounce off me
like Superman shedding gunfire.
Let the bullets fall like rain to the ground.
I would shrug it off to let him know
he can't touch me or those I love.

Today the only pain I feel within
I cause myself with doubts
and no matter how hard I try
to again find the child I once was
the conclusions are the same.
My Clark Kent lies in an open empty grave
and my Superman only exists as ashes
spread from then to now
on breezes of regret and shame.

Back then I believed in superheroes.

<u>My Letter To You</u>

I always feel you there within me.
That unforgiving itch I can't scratch.
Each attempt to rid myself of you
grows more useless.

It dilutes the feeble whisper of happiness
just under my faked public happy thoughts.
You are the voice from the nothingness
tempting me to give in, embrace you,
Stockholm syndrome for the corrosive entity inside.

I stand firm every time my skin is pierced
just to prove that I am not weak.
But to who? You, me, them?
Does it really matter?
As days pass, forever, one after another,
I am here and will always be
along for the ride
It is no choice of mine.

You live in this cell with me.
Never getting out,
never escaping.
I'll sit here, you and I
chained together to this cell
and no matter how weak you make me
I will keep searching for the strength
to simply escape.

Sand

Sand pours in the seconds of infinity.
I drown beneath the sands of time.
The hour glass my prison.
Unable to break the glass
despite it being an emergency.

My childhood slid like sand
between lubricated fingers.
Desperately grasping at nostalgic ghosts.
Trying hard but never reaching,
never finding justice
for the untimely death of
a childhood's innocence.

Instead I was trapped on
this forever treadmill of hardship.
Running down pain
in exchange for distracted survival
while searching by hope
for those lost sands of history.

Yet I am still drowning.
Unable to catch my breath.
Maybe, if I stopped holding it in
and gave in to the fact that I'm drowning,
this world, this life, this hope
would be the light I go into
and the sands would no longer drown me.

Thoughts

Lose
   your mind
just
  let it
           go

if it comes back
   embrace it
     laugh
                 cry
       RAGE
  fuck it!!

and then

toss   it
       back out
before
your mind spoils
     its new found

        freedom

A Novel Observation

Today you can walk down any street,
cruise any highway,
look in any window
and see nothing but unwritten novels
on the virgin canvas of the human spirit
sacrificed by illiteracy and ignorance,
epics that would make Gilgamesh

as sweet and unimportant as the Three Little Pigs.

The truth is children no longer sit and listen
to stories from their grandparents
of times when things were different,
when things were "better",
before technology, terrorists, politicians and Hollywood
fucked things up for this generation,
the next and the foreseeable future of humanity.

What I would give to see tears
and smiles on the youngest of us.
Just one singular sensational moment
for that brief flicker to appear in a little one's eyes
and then extinguish itself
before eventually fueling the fire
that burns through their fears
to ignite immortal passions and dreams.
A childhood fable exploding to life, becoming reality.

Afterwards you will come to one conclusion,
and only that one, simple, undeniable solution:
Things are not as they should be.
The machine is broken.
Life is broken.
Pinocchio's dreams have come true
giving away hopes and dreams to be a human boy,
forever living in a prison of strings
spun by our own mistakes, fears and ignorance.

Welcome to Toledo

Taxicabs slow to flagged cash,
hungry transport service uncaged
like greedy monkey boy bellhops.
Crack the window and let the night breeze flood in
from an anonymous world becoming more anonymous.

Toledo doesn't know your name,
Toledo never cared.
Toledo is just a city in name,
a city built on the backs of crumbling workers
and strained pensions.

The cell phone cries a wakeup call
as a symphony to a singular man.
Tomorrow's mirror stares back
as these eyes glare blindly
at the royalty of rare crystal clear reception.
It's all in the balcony view from the other side,
but Romeo never knew Toledo.

Caesar would be proud of this city state,
Shakespearean futures now today's tragedies.
This living, breathing, cement and tear organism
is each heart bleeding within its confines.

Welcome to Toledo.

Toledo At Night

The last time I saw Toledo at night
the hospital had been my prison.
I had broken free to flea

back home through the heart of the city
driving through a maze of utopian Urbana.

A pharmacy catches my eye.
I'm drawn to its flickering neon sign
"Open 24 hours",
a silent heavy metal ballad
screaming as a floodlight,
beaconing to hopeless junkies,
soulless prostitutes,
and the destitute homeless
looking for their own endless highs.
A man sits just outside of the entrance
covering his face to hide warm saline tears.
I couldn't tell you why.
He struggles to stand.
His dead man's stance unforgettable
like his love for canned dead meat
and strings attached to a glorified rectum
that empties with a swift tug.

Garbage dump city
reeking of broken lives.
The city that never dreams
just collects those of others.
This is a city that sleeps
where it can, with who it wants.
No bed of its own,
no love to keep company.
This city is dead at 3am
when the mind is chirping.
Only women of the night
stand hands in their pockets
where they stash their belongings
like forever and ash,
condoms and birth control,

and can no longer see the way.

I turned on the news tonight
to catch a glimpse of yesterday's Toledo.
Every channel covers the same story.
Three little boys are still missing.
Surely the worse has happened.
Three of Toledo's youngest lives now taken,
surely snuffed out by their own father
and every day there seems to be more bad
overshadowing the city's abundance of good.
Death and life keep trying to clash,
caught in the middle
hope lays wounded.
This is why I rarely watch news anymore
and we all know the newspaper is a joke.
Every now and then
Toledo proves us all wrong
with the laughing of children
living in gangland under ramshackle roofs,
veterans putting their lives on the line
in their neighborhood's war on drugs
and the smiles from every plate filled
at the Cherry Street Mission.

The last time I saw Toledo at night
was the first time I really looked at Toledo.

Questions

Every life,
yours, mine,
ours,
is a reality

29

born and constructed
from an infinite number of questions...
None of which have answers,
just letters and syllables arranged in patterns
that flow from the mind
meaning what we want them to mean
and ending up as nothing more than
the rhythmic rhyming sound
of bongos on our eardrums.

Rat-a-tat-tat
Rat-a-tat-tat.
There will never be any meaning to that.

The number of questions build.
The pressure blinds us to the view
that all we have left is garbage and clutter
where our answers are supposed to be.

Anxiety And Randomness

In this self-induced mental fog
I breathe in
medicated trying to relieve
and deceive the anxiety I feel.

Nuclear bomb like thoughts
heavily dropping from above
have me thinking about how
deep the anxiety of my anxiety is.
You feel me?

I'm having anxiety about
how much anxiety I'm having.

It's unforgiving.
How do I stop the anxiety that's building when
I'm having anxiety about controlling the anxiety.

I could lay down but the anxiety
about not dealing with this anxiety
will keep me awake.
I guess I will put these feelings into letters,
then those letters into words
placed upon this page
and let the anxiety escape into the universe
from my mind into this world.
Then my anxiety will be
all of yours
to be anxious about.

The Everyman

The every man from here and there,
those disabled factory vets
or the never 9 to 5 pushovers,
sweep the rubble, the dirt and filth
of the concrete ghetto into their heads.
With hands made of industrial inhuman tools
they scrape away at the bowels of humanity
finding pieces of shit and pride deep
under their fingernails on each bleeding finger.

The everyman seeks what can't be found.
A truth hidden where the classes of kings and pimps
feign fear and truth behind happiness.
The everyman are blind but experience it
because they know the burden of occupation
and the reality of false hope.

They are the no ones,
the clout of a cog in a machine.
Each one quietly toils and burns away
in hellfire and the shadows of mindless ether,
which some think is the chemical equivalent of oil
while others know the only equal to it is blood.

The everyman dreams of levers and ash,
smoke stacks and metal, life and death,
and then awaken to a world they built.

Street Gutter Living

The streets create a substance
in their gutters like reflections
of a concrete culture wasting the wasted.
The filth lived and tasted
scratching for forgiveness
and screaming for greatness.
We walk the cracks of our own fears.
We sleep in paper bags like atmospheres.
Gathering an existence
we hunt for more resistance
tamed like creatures
creating life-like measures
living in homes of street gutters.

Tiles And Titles

The world is made with tiles and titles,
baked in claymation golems
and asphalt packaged idols.

Freedom evolved from these truths,
became glass concrete,
shattered into fiery dream cutting shrapnel,
burnt down to ashen glitter steel
and laid to rest plastered in Paris.
The world was made of tiles and titles
and in the end only dirt remains
blowing forever dry in a tearless wake

Revealing Buried Truths

All of the dirt has blown away
revealing buried truths to unknown
invaders from another time,
another place,
another reality,
another poem
No lines are drawn,
only the tracking beacon signals
"here".

As I wait trying to understand,
a question comes to mind:
If there is a signal to here,
is there a signal to nowhere?
I try to find one,
any sound,
any word,
any vision,
but I can't see through the walls
created by my thoughts
of the fallen financial fortress twins
or
the wilted flowers of Columbine's garden

or
the two lost young souls
of 1993 and 1994 Holland Ohio.
One life taken
   on snowstorm cloaked train tracks
   crossing into the afterlife painlessly.
The other life
   a victim of a carefree summer vacation.
   Started with cabin living and family bonding
   only to end with a Devil's Lake
   of scalene tears.

I leave these thoughts tongue tied,
a soulless monotone machine
needing oiled with painful words
that become poetry,
my living ghost dance
of unburied tile truths,
and this ghost dance
is private.

The City Below

This city made noir
lay below big brother exchanges
hidden in the filth,
hidden in the infinite unseen,
transpired in gutter peace
and trashed tranquility.

After several awakenings
they had all become used to
a city of unrecognizable beauty
and the idea of a future
of industrial quiet commands.

An apocalyptic city
comfortable from birth
in a mirage,
in an illusion
of the logic of past years
when wars against fantasy
led to lives of expectation
and humanity challenged itself to change
with false flag motives
that spoke a simple truth:
They wanted it this way.

It Is What It Is

The real deals can't be found
in sharpened Blade newspaper pages
or turpentine antiseptic news bits
from fragile glass city puppeteers.
True life happens in the unseen,
It is what it is.

When dark alleys grow darker
as a low cost apartment below emits screams
from a cracked out mom
dangling baby from one arm
and shooting crack with the other
before fill-in dad hits her for dinner being cold.
It is what it is.

And the beggar down the way that heard her cry
begs for just one bite more
but the dimes he collects
won't help him escape from the grave
in the alley where red roses lie in wait.
It is what it is.

And next door a party is in full swing,
DJ puts on Ice cube,
wolves find a sheep
and the grinding commences.
One dances with her as the other
slips a ketamine surprise into her rum and coke.
In minutes one becomes many
and the monsters converge on their prey.
A rave to the grave.
It is what it is.

And, as the world continues its blind midnights,
bullies in black hoodies
ride shotgun on their bikes
carrying knives, carrying a gun,
absolving family matters
by robbing their uncle's corner store.
Smokes and dollars, blood and bondage.
The ghetto bird rides high.
It is what it is.

Blood, sweat, tears and crack.
Real world poetry in motion.
It is what it is.

Hard Times

Hard times
Gritting teeth
Breaking down
Ground up
Desperate measures

Rebuilding the

Fallen world
From dust
From dirt
From nothing

Finding the
Way out
Through Hell
And back

Rough circumstances
Breeds hardness
Culls darkness
Creates scars
To
Remind us.

Cold hearts
Keep beating
Rebuilding us
Through surviving
Desperate measures
And
Hard times.

Plastic City Skylines

We ride programmed vehicles of thought
on synthetic silicon roads always
"under construction".
Finding our way home is seemingly impossible
without the appropriate app guiding us
to titanium skyscrapers demanding our presence.

Shadows of the inorganic skyline of a plastic city.
The labels of our designer thoughts
read "wash well"
and
"Made in China".
Information highways paved in digital concrete
and pot-holed fiber optics
where, in the end, we end up alone
surrounded by digitized no-ones
without a home.

Captain America Carries A Glock

Captain America carries a Glock,
the new world order's new world justice.
Shoot first, ask questions later,
let God sort out the innocent.

Captain America pulls the trigger.
Easier than it should be.
Each bullet painting liberty's constitution
        with rounds blood red
inked from preprogrammed enemies
        of the white knight
Rounds scatter brains out
        on false sky blue canvases.
Heaven is full, its gates are locked
and Hell doesn't seem to give a shit.

Captain America isn't blind.
He keeps his mighty shield shined
as bright as a halo
        and as red as hellfire.
His puppet eyes see what he's meant to see...

tattered genes,
rage against machines
needing to be put down.
Too bad what goes around
usually never comes back around.
We don't want to think about it,
don't want to talk about it
and that's how it all began.

Captain American is an artist.
His new exhibit opened at the museum of art.
Crowds gather, the public flood the halls
trying to get a glimpse
of their hero's blood stained lives
        framed on display.

Captain America carries a Glock
and has never lost Russian roulette.
Life is a game of expression
painted by violence
 and righteous perfection.
His missions are always completed.

Captain America - the new 21st century super soldier
forged by our own blind, mute hands,
The flawless warrior of a flawed people.

God bless America.

Pride's Letter To Society

Society, you sit there in your nothingness,
deep within a cerebral closet,
locked inside by self-doubt and fear.

Your only companion a sea of darkness
slowly swallowing and suffocating.
Deeper and deeper
becoming an illusionary construct
to those on the outside looking in,
a fortress of perceived normalcy for the blind.
The worse lies are those
we tell ourselves.

Lonely,
they say perception is reality
and the reality is that you, society,
are made of broken dreams and pigeon-holed views
of what you and I are,
what we have become....
what
have
we
become.
The answer always seems
to come down to pride.

Society, does it matter what you think
when the truth of who you are
lies behind the many masks
hiding your broken soul,
behind the unbreakable shell
now a coffin for your heart.
Does it matter what you think
if you cannot admit who you are.

Society, respect is pride.
Lessons learned, lessons earned.
Sexuality, just one shadow cast aside,
illuminated through education,
shattered by truth,

burned by insightful soul.
Exception fueled toleration,
turned to hate's ashes
blown away by winds of change.

Society, freedom is not won with tears alone,
but with the reasons for those tears.
Let them fall free and fiercely,
the tears of you and me,
black, white,
straight, gay,
Christian, Muslim,
tens, hundreds. thousands, millions,
forming one raging river,
then melding into an ocean of one,
an ocean of strength,
an ocean of tolerance,
an ocean of pride,
an ocean of freedom.

Truth Poetica

It seems that revolution is the new fad.
From Paris to iPads,
paparazzi addictions of the common man
taking the backseat
to a once buried,
currently surfacing reality.
Now it's anti-labor and ayatollahs
feeding our chemical needs.
Abysmal void sucking down nothingness
screaming to be filled by empty syringe.
Make me whole!
Shot after shot,

steroids for the masses
shrinking our testicles with each round.
Making dicks so small
that we no longer worry
about fucking ourselves over
or being screwed by the idiot next to us.
I guess that could be a good thing though.
It just depends on if you're at the receiving end
and lately it seems like most of us have been.
On CNN the crowds keep gathering,
chanting, marching, doing what needs to be done
for one purpose only:
to express what they believe
in order to change their worlds
from black and blue
to gold and platinum.
Maybe desire is revolution's true form
and, as a poet, I desire for tomorrow.
These words will make sure I get there.

Painting Liberty

Health care, marijuana, flip-flops,
conservative signs of the Apocalypse.
The anti-Christ sits at a computer
in boxers that cover the naked truth
while waging a holy war.
His vision is sparked by syllables,
words and lines of poetic essence
fed by societal combustion
exploding onto the screen
as common sense in an age of idiocy.

I slide my fingers over the keyboard

and begin to type, black on white,
on a canvas of hopes and ideals.
A colorblind Picasso attempting
to master the Mona Lisa.
Every line inside waiting
to come alive.

We live in a gray world
amongst gray lives
existing solely on gray morals
as red innocent blood
is spilled by black hearts
for just a little more green
in their pockets.

One word, and then another,
bringing truth to light:
a homeless child on Cherry Street,
a gangbanger on Erie.
Seen, but never seen,
a poet's calling in the flesh.

Red, white, blue, purple, green,
We are all poets of the mind
living in technicolor dreams
and painting liberty
in a colorless world.

I Am An American

I am an American.
I live life to my own definition.
I hate out of pride.
I love out of compassion.

I try to be honest
and
I die.
I am an American.
I believe in faith.
I believe in freedom.
I believe in people.
I am an American.
I am told to trust our government.
I have only put my trust in my family and justice.

I am an American,
but America is falling.
I am an American,
but people are selfish and greedy here.
I am an American,
but our government is filthy and diseased.
A crack whore turning tricks for economic stability,
right and left,
on both sides
I am an American,
but everybody wants life all expenses paid.
Nobody tries to earn it anymore.
I am an American,
but where are all of the other Americans?
When Katrina and Ike hit.
When the economy turned to shit.
When a child dies of starvation
on streets paved with gold.
When our leaders betray us
only to live on our blood and tears.
When we have sent thousands of our children
into a lie, a WMD of our making.

I am an American,
but who will stand against the enemy within,

against the liars who want to be
        seen at any cost,
    against the leaders who have deceived us
        no matter the body count,
    against these liars that want to screw us
        again and again.
I am an American,
but I can't do it alone.
I need to see some common sense and compassion.
I know there are others who see the truths as I do.
I am an American.
I want America to truly live.
I want our families to never worry again
    about their next paycheck,
    about how they will eat today,
    about finding a way to pay the doctor
        when a child is ill.
I want our President to be truth.

I am an American.

I Will Never Write A Political Poem

I refuse to write a political poem.
It blinds your idea of me,
                of who I am,
                of what I'm about.
You will think I am a revolutionist,
speaking yet saying nothing
sound pollution, call the EPA.
If this is true
then it means poems are petitions,
                picket signs,
                the first stone thrown,

45

the blood of soldiers.

We put onto paper
in invisible ink:
What we thought is right is wrong,
                true is untrue.
Words like these are volunteers to genocide,
                givers to the poor,
                blind to passions,
                deaf in need.
No matter what is written:
Poetry will not cure AIDS.
Poetry will not defend the fallen.
Poetry will not stop the injustices worldwide.
Poetry is words spat from the lips and tongues
in the saliva of a mute man.
Words in the form of ideas
impressing idiots through vocabulary.
If I spoke them to you,
these words would invoke
claps and cheers
and then fade into walls
disappearing from this room.

What we need are sniper poems,
poems that make us bleed
without a single word spoken
making a point
that will never be forgotten.

No, I will not write a political poem
because these words will never
be worth a damn.

Speaking Of Wisconsin Cheese

Politicians have gathered in swarms
like flies multiplying on bloody excrement
made of the People for the People,
reality's Soilent Green.
Their chewed up freedoms and digested rights
laying in the federal toilet bowl
ready to be flushed once more
after diligently wiping their own untouchable asses
with unearned, stolen greenbacks.

Smiling from their porcelain thrones,
proud of the stink they made.
Tear gas for the masses that show up and remain.
Sitting, watching, doing nothing more.
Nothing comes from the slowing, stagnant protests,
only the sight of freedom swirling....
down, down, down.

Wisconsin government cheese and American cheddar
sharpened by greed and sweat.
"Times are uh changin'"
Growing day after day,
the lactose intolerance of the unknown worker
is causing unending, unspeakable pain
that we all end up feeling.
The only cure they turn to
is the fraud enshrined porcelain dream eater
filled over and over.

The cycle never ends and with every flush
the tears of public cries flow.
These rivers of tears,
torrents flowing underground
building, strengthening, flowing into one another

becoming one, becoming strong,
becoming unstoppable, untamable,
getting louder, more fierce, deafening.
Until it rumbles and quakes,
shaking golden palaces at their very foundation
and finally spewing forth into daylight.
A force of nature to be reckoned with
known simply and collectively as a union named
We, the People.

An American Truth

Change is constant
yet we demand it
from politics and politicians
like a corner crack dealer.
A dime bag costing our freedom
                        our hopes
                        our dreams.

We are told "Vote or Die!"
We vote and thousands die.
Promised a better tomorrow
with just a pull on the lever.
A single solitary action,
a message goes out
texting the executioner
                "bring the noose".
            It's ok, it's American made.
An American made noose
        around American made necks
        killing American made thoughts and dreams
        becoming the American made way.

They say the right to vote is a gift
and the outcome is our receipt.
The last time I checked
the signs on voting day
all read "Nonrefundable".

Opiate Dreams

The large adult-proof bottle
beckons me as a siren's call.
Sailing in a sea of pain
the contents are the answer,
allowing me to get lost
in its tides until I crash,
happiness shatters
and the nightmares flood back in.

I struggle to open a bottle
that I know any ten year old can.
The white pills fall
into my unsteady hand.
Courting me, glittering in my mind
like fireworks downtown
on the fourth of July
as it enters me,
absorbing into every cell
in my broken body.

Shortly it begins to dance in my brain
from one neurotransmitter to another,
doing the tango from lobe to lobe,
salsa dancing from brainstem to spinal cord
leaving disappointment in its wake.
Minutes of synthetic perfection

amongst an eternity of debility.

Soon reality fades into chemical dreams.
I sleep alone, as I always have,
afraid to compromise the euphoria
that doesn't feel so euphoric anymore.
Someone is always killing me
in my opiate dreams,
effortless and unapologetic,
a faceless enigma
I know all too well.
With my last breath
I wake up.
The manufactured pain relief gone.
Once more unable to move,
the only thing I feel is pain.
I slowly turn around
and see the large adult-proof bottle
beckoning me,
calling me back into my opiate dreams.

Dreams Of Nuclear Napalm

As a child I would lay in bed
and dream of pumpkin pie and napalm.
My innocence was lost forever
amongst forever nothings
sent as serialized nightly visions..
Little orphan Annie raped
by experiences never felt,
never seen, never alive,
just..
never.

She would continue on oblivious,
afraid of nothing.
Too bad it all comes
to her as nothing
packaged in bloody Versace
and Sachs 5th Avenue somethings.

Anthrax and diamonds
forged with the crushing hammer
called idiocracy taking form of democracy
and cooled in the geyser of hate
that will set the world on fire.
It was nuclear napalm
erupting from a radioactive wet dream.

Little orphan Annie rides by in fallout skies
on her shotgun vibrator set on high.
Boom! Boom! Pleasure for the masses!
Let her scream! Let us all scream!
And then after the fallout and hate,
after the nuclear napalm and shotgun dreams,
there is silence and innocence.

Toy Soldiers (The Children)

They exchange babies for bullets.
Trained little toy soldiers,
just wind them up
and knock them down.
Kindergarten Marines with runny noses
passing on sicknesses to enemy soldiers.
Anti-aircraft slingshots
and bottle rocket submarine launched missiles.
Entire crews of boogeymen lay dying.

They call themselves pirates,
sword in one hand,
pacifier in the other.
Prisoners of their customs.

We are warned of evil terrorists
and defended by a kaleidoscope of colors.
Oh look! It's a red day.
Get to your bunkers,
grab your automatics.
Terror hits home
as rattles and binkies
and five year olds plant i.e.d.s like tulips
watering the harsh soil
with tears and blood of American mothers.
The mission is all that matters.
Only some of their babies
will come home.

Mission codenamed: Murder.
Don't mind the brightly colored ribbons
in her hair
or the muddied pigskin
in his hands,
they are only remote controlled assassins
masked as preschoolers
by protégé programmers
whose only goal in life
is making weapons of mass destruction easy.
A dirty bomb with pigtails and a bottle.
After all it's hard to kill a target
when it's teething
and justifying an explanation
for the use of deadly force
when the victim is only three.

Suicide bombers, suicide infants,
suicide toddlers crawling for the first time
on their knees in front of tanks and convoys
like marbles rolling across tabletops.
C-4 packed diapers worn perfectly
never to be changed.
Blowing away fellow toy soldiers.
Fallen down never
to be picked up once more.

The reality of today
is trust is dead,
truth is dead,
innocence is dead.
You can't trust a toddler
to not be packing heat.
A clip or two
hidden by a cute smile
and you're afraid to walk
down the street to the park,
scared you will see a little boy in Batman
or little girl princess
strapped with dynamite,
enough explosives to level a playground,
waiting to see the surprise in your eyes
then pressing the button.
Back and forth,
like the swing set creaking nearby,
but much deadlier.

These days educating our children
seems unnecessary
when they don't need
to learn how to count to ten.
Ten seconds would be more than enough time
to kill you or I,

their mother, our fathers,
teachers, doctors,
priests and Buddha himself.
No, they have no need for school itself.
No need for math, social studies, language or art.
No need with lives predestined
by the hand of the toymakers,
our own hands.

The ten digits on our palms
assemble the bombs,
cock the guns,
wind up each toy soldier,
aim and let go.

Aim..

Let go..

Each little life we have aimed
at adult targets
and let go,
washing blood from adult hands
but no matter how hard we scrub,
how much we wash,
the blood is eternal.
A reminder of each and every
little toy soldier.

For Those That Will Forever Be Faded But Never Forgotten

People, as a whole, are bad at most things,
good at some
and great at very few.
These days all talent resides in the art of not caring,

It's times when I'm placid and monochromatic
that I get the shock of reality at its most painful.
It hits me as electricity at its most primal
and starts traveling from synapse to synapse
as Frankenstein nerves find life
supercharged by never felt pure emotion.
A tear forms.... it all goes heavy.

I'm flushed, feeling strapped to this electric chair
where leaning the wrong way or thinking the wrong thought
can set it off,
a deluge of regrettable hurt
leading to another pill ...and another tear.

Spinning head, shouldering through it.
I must keep going. I just must.
Then I look behind me.

The small footprints left on the ground,
Dirt holed pathways on my heart
are ever gradually fading,
distracting me with both the words and colors I inhale and exhale.
Blocking my soul expression, my life.

I try to quit thinking.
A cliché that never works.

Then, too late...
Gone.

Another away.
Again.
......

As each letter forms each word,
thoughts, feelings and memories
begin to leak through the silent maelstrom I call a soul,
and lightning brands send piercing bolts into me deeper,
more painful than ever.

I see colors cracking the dam of darkness...
A drip, a stream, a river, an ocean.

Slowly it all starts washing away.
All but the faded memories.
All but the faded footprints.

The Yellow Submarine Bus Ride

Lost in day dream haze
somewhere in my mind,
I see a man aged too prematurely
sitting for the yellow submarine bus.
As soon as it pulls up
his arthritic legs unstiffen.
Snap, crackle, pop, walks
finds his new seat,
and then pop, crackle, snap,
arthritic grasp retakes it's hold.
His eyes devour the city passing by
like smothered blueberry pancakes
but the syrup is suspicious

and dreams have slid from his plate.
Fallen, they have left only a tasty, ugly stain
on an already ugly floor.

As the bus comes to an assigned stop
he watches a poet named Jesus
at the Greyhound bus stop
giving away paper stigmata
and old hope.
His hands are holy batons.
His hands are torn rope
His voice is damaged and rusty
as if he has eaten only nails and loss,
left his youth held at gunpoint
and raped in an alley.
The same alley where
he screwed a noun
and downed a vowel.
I want to embrace him
for his lifetime as a ghost
and see his smile become more
than just a curl of smoke.

The bus reaches its last stop.
Time for both the man and I
to depart for home.
This experienced has made me
into the dirty bruised peach I washed
in a woman's public bathroom.
Hell, it may have been wrong,
but it was necessary
and Hell has a lot to say some days,
especially these days.

Maybe everything is simpler
on the yellow submarine bus.

Finding The Way

I walk the road alone
    wondering where I am headed.
I know where I am,
    I just don't know when to stop.

I see all the streets,
    all the people living their lives.
Maybe one day I won't be walking
    and I'll be just like them.
Happy where they stand.

However I am here
    walking down another street,
    this one busier.
And I find that no matter
    how far I walk
    here is not where I need to be.

    I need to leave.

Haikus

Sand Castles

When this storm passes,
walls have fallen, ashes will
become sand castles.

Testimonials In Haiku: Truths in Reality #1

Sometimes our dreams end
disappearing into smoke
called our daily lives.

Testimonials In Haiku: Truths in Reality #2

Awake and asleep
meld together into one
fantasia made real.

Testimonials In Haiku: Truths in Reality #3

I still try to dream,
but mostly I stay awake
because dreams will lie.

Testimonials In Haiku: Truths in Reality #4

Lies, though, can be truths.
It is our realities,
not dreams, that decide.

Testimonials In Haiku: Truths in Reality #5

Once I dreamed I walked.
My feet fell on solid ground
when my eyes would close.

Testimonials In Haiku: Truths in Reality #6

These days I still wish
to make dreams real, lies less cruel,
and hope more truthful.

Testimonials In Haiku: Truths in Reality #7

Cruelty and truth,
the hell born two headed snake,
both deal equal pain.

Testimonials In Haiku: Truths in Reality #8

Pain is a teacher.
It tells us who we once were
and who we are now.

At Last A Little Humor In Poetry

Holy Trouble

Today, sitting in front of my computer screen,
I heard the voice of God.
There was no mistaking who it was
with that tremble inducing sigh
and the thunderous "Hey shit head!"
that followed.
In only the way God can,
he told me to stop writing poetry.
"It's a waste, get a fucking job."
I turned around and yelled
to him to stop bitching,
but he just kept on.
What was I supposed to do?
This is God after all.
So I lowered my hands
away from the keyboard,
giving into Him
just to get Him off my ass.
He smiled, turned,
said thank you and left.
Right away this shit head
put his hands back to the keyboard
and began typing this.
Not even God can stop
a poet's words.

Facebook Sexuality

If sex was a status update we'd all be sluts
leaving comments that say nothing
to get each other off,
such as
"lol lmao fyi atm xyz".
We don't need to look closer
at a newly uploaded pic
only to see their pants around their ankles
as we trip over our dsl connection.
It's alright,
there is still foreplay.
That's it, move the mouse gently.
Ask a question.
"What's your favorite food?"
Respond to their comment.
"That sounds great!"
and
"Lol you're so funny!".
I know, it drives you insane.

Without warning
they take it to the next level.
The chat opens up.
An arousing game of 20 questions
is about to be played
or is it 30?
I stroke my ego
as you record a live bulleted webcam
for your newsfeed.
Every click drives me insane.
Facebook never felt so sexy.

But we must be careful.
There are so many viruses

and other sexually technological diseases,
STDs,
on Facebook.
Before long your screen will go black,
your hard drive will blister.
Make sure to wear a firewall at all times.
If you do catch something
don't worry,
Dr. Norton can sort this out,
his anti-virus protection is cheap
in this digital age.

After we are all dressed up,
our files in order,
we can go on a date,
out for a byte
guaranteed to raise and stimulate
your satirical libido.
We will spam our favorite places,
YouTube and Facebook.
My status will be my favorite pickup line.
We will begin to leave one another wall posts.
You, then I, sharing and getting closer.
Our union becoming more electrifying,
the typed text like our tongues
kissing through introductory messages
and wall responses.

Our static lives are far from introduced.
Photos and blogs shake hands
and one can only question
the validity of the knowledge.
Who are you really?
And who am I?
The answers encrypted
in a language only known

to my core processor.

A newly versed paranoia
we quickly depart each other's company.
One click, maybe two,
and it's over,
like waking up the next morning
after too much alcohol
and not enough sobriety.
Treading lightly,
tapping the keys ever so gently
so as not to wake the other up.

We gather ourselves for the day,
turn on our respective c.p.u.'s
and reflect on l.e.d. memories.
We do not stop to consider,
we act.

Your favorite food is?

Stalled Ecstasy

Have you ever had to take a piss so bad it burns?
You feel it welling up in your abdomen,
fiery and unforgiving.
Every water-like sound, every jostle,
every single move you make
adding to your agony
and your growing inability to hold it off.

Then it's time, holding it is no longer an option.
Do you try to hold it,
or rudely run off leaving your friends behind?

Of course you run
like a spanked ferret looking for payback
to the nearest stall you can find.
If you're a guy
going solo is the key
to the whole experience.
But if you're a woman
you would most likely bring that friend along.
I've never understood the feminine need
to invite their friends to the peepee party.
Just as long as they don't share the party favors.

Once you're in your favorite position
you unzip.
That zzzzt sound a heavenly bugle
ushering in incoming salvation.
Finally you whip it out,
or sit,
I'm not judging,
and let loose that hot,
yellow, steaming river of pleasure.
It burns a bit at first
but following that slight pain
is pure ecstasy,
orgasmic porno blowjob moaning ecstasy.
It feels so good that you could swear
Jenna Jameson was down there,
yet you hope not
because you definitely wouldn't want to pee on her.
Unless you would,
which is rather nasty,
but again I'm not judging.

As it winds down, the stream a mere trickle,
the sputter of your neighbors 1971 VW Wagon,
sputter, squirt, sputter, the end,

and, although that feeling of awe
unequal to any high
is now gone,
you know that it's just a few beers,
a pot of coffee,
or some cans of Mountain Dew
and a couple of unbearable hours of waiting away.

65874892R00044

Made in the USA
Lexington, KY
28 July 2017